FIFTEEN WALKS FROM
AMBLESIDE AND GRASMERE

PAUL BUTTLE

Published by
amadorn

I would like to thank the following people for the help they have given me producing this guide: Lesley Blacklock, Pat Clark, Lynne Denny, David Pitchford, Trevor Wright, and Pádraig Ó Cíobháin for "an cúpla focal".

ISBN 0 9513717 4 6

First published May, 1991
Reprinted February 1992, October 1992, May 1993, March 1995, February 1997, February 1998, June 1999, July 2000, June 2002 (with minor changes and additions), January 2004, July 2005, February 2008, May 2009

Published by Amadorn, 18 Brewery Lane, Keswick, Cumbria.
Typeset by Ferguson Bros. (Printers) Ltd., Keswick, Cumbria.
Maps by Gelder, Much Dewchurch, Herefordshire.
Printed by Nuffield Press, Abingdon, Oxfordshire

CONTENTS

INTRODUCTION

The fifteen walks in this guide present a wide choice from modest low level walks to very challenging high level walks. Probably not all the walks will be of interest to every walker, but hopefully most people will find six or seven that are.

Order of walks

I have ordered the walks, at least within each category; low, intermediate and high, as much as I could judge, by the amount of effort involved. Thus the easiest walks roughly come first and the hardest last. This way of ordering the walks I hope will serve some purpose in helping you to decide which one to choose.

Timing of walks

This is always difficult to judge as it depends not only on an individual's fitness but also on his or her predilection for taking breaks. The ' Suggested times' in this book therefore are just a rough guide. They are calculated on the basis of 'Naismith's rule' allowing one hour for every three miles covered and one hour for every thousand feet ascended. This way of calculating the time of a walk does not allow for any stops, picnics or philosophical musings. If you are prone to any of these activities you should adapt the 'suggested' timing of the walks accordingly.

Choice of Maps.

A map is essential on the fells and even on low level walks it is best to be with one. The Ordnance Survey produce two different scale maps that can be used in conjunction with this guide:-

Landranger Series Sheet 90, scale 1:50,000
All the walks in this guide are covered by this map though not the whole of the Lake District - three other maps are needed (sheets 89, 96 and 97). Formerly one needed only the "one inch" O.S. Tourist Map to tramp the whole Lakeland fells, but regrettably production of this map was discontinued around the start of this century.

Explorer Series, English Lakes, scale 1:25,000.
These are amazingly detailed maps. As they show all the field boundaries they are definitely the best maps to use on low level walks. There are four separate maps covering the Lake District; North West, North East, South West and South East. This is one of their drawbacks. They are a bit expensive to buy all together. They are also a bit bulky as well if you carry all four of them around at the same time. The walks in this guide actually cover all four sheets, though you could just about get away without using the North West map as only the High White Stones walk clips into the corner of it. A minor 'fault' with these maps which you should be careful to look out for when using them is their rather deceptive representation of footpaths. This arises because rights of way are represented with prominent thick green dashed lines. This is fine when these rights of way exist as footpaths but not infrequently they do not exist as paths at all. More reliable are the feint black dashed lines, which don't stand out too well. These lines represent footpaths which are not rights of way. Their representation of actual existing footpaths, though, is remarkably accurate and surprisingly comprehensive.

Public transport

The start of all the walks in this guide, if they don't actually begin from Ambleside or Grasmere, are reachable from either centre by using public transport. The final walk in this guide actually relies on the use of public transport as it is a linear walk. There are two main bus services that connect Ambleside and Grasmere to the walks in this book:-

Lancaster to Keswick Service 555/6
This service follows the A591 through the Lake District and connects Ambleside with Grasmere and both those places with Stanah, at the northern end of Thirlmere, the start of the Helvellyn walk. In the summer this service runs usually every hour. Outside the summer season it runs about every two hours.

Ambleside to Dungeon Ghyll Service 516
This service connects Ambleside to Elterwater and the Old and New Dungeon Ghyll Hotels in Great Langdale.

In Ambleside buses pick up in Kelsick Road opposite the library. To get there, walk south from the information centre in the centre of Ambleside and after passing the Post Office take the first turn right on to King Street which joins Kelsick Road. In Grasmere buses going north pick up opposite Sam Read's bookshop. Buses going south pick up opposite Heaton Cooper's Gallery. Timetables for all the above services are usually well displayed at the relevant bus stops. In addition for some years now Stagecoach in Cumbria, which operates these services, have produced a very useful timetable brochure which is obtainable at all information centres and usually on all their buses as well from April to October. For phone enquiries telephone 0871 200 22 33.

Safety on the fells

Most of the walks in this guide are serious high level fellwalks, make sure therefore you are properly equipped if you go on them, especially if you are walking in the winter season or in late autumn or early spring, when the weather conditions on the fell tops can be very different to the weather in the valleys. Ensure you have a waterproof or windproof outer jacket, sturdy boots with a good sole pattern, hat and gloves and spare warm clothing, a comfortable day sack, food and something to drink, a compass, torch and whistle. To check on Lake District weather conditions phone 08700 550 575.

Is obair chruaidh a bheith ag siúl suas cnoic ach is duaisuila
fós do Shasanach na focail seo a léamh .

Walk 1 # THE ROTHAY CIRCUIT

Distance	8¹/₂ miles
Total feet of ascent	500 feet
Suggested time	3 hours
Starting point	Ambleside Market Cross (NY 376 046)

Rothay is the name of the river flowing from Grasmere to Ambleside, hence the name of this walk, though it could well be called the Wordsworth Walk, as it passes within a hundred yards of his grave in Grasmere in St Oswald's churchyard and also past two of his Lakeland homes; Rydal Mount, where he lived almost half his lifetime, and the more famous Dove Cottage, both of which are open to the public. There is no doubting though that if Wordsworth were able to come back to life today he would be horrified at how much Lakeland has changed, particularly this part of it where he lived for so much of his life. The modern A591 has done much to destroy the rural peace this Lakeland valley once possessed. However this walk, at least in parts, helps to recapture a sense of that more tranquil past.

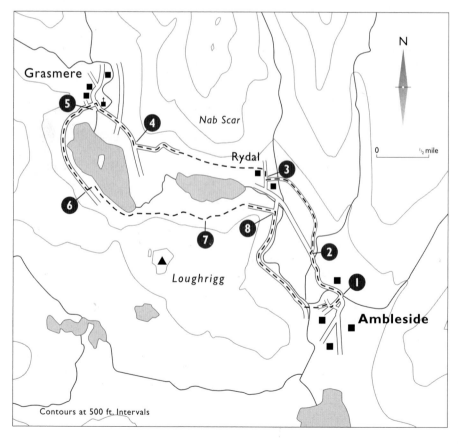

1   Follow the main road out of Ambleside northwards towards Grasmere. After leaving the conurbation of the town and crossing over a small bridge, turn right off the road on to what looks to be a private driveway, with some imposing cast-iron gates, to Rydal Hall. A public footpath sign nearby however indicates that the driveway is in fact a right of way. ($^1/_2$ mile)

2   Follow the driveway through the attractive grounds of the Hall up to the Hall itself. Here the driveway runs round the back of the Hall and joins a surfaced roadway running uphill through the hamlet of Rydal. Where there might be any doubt near to the Hall as to which trackway to follow, a series of prominent footpath signs clearly indicate the correct route to take. (1 mile)

3   On reaching the road turn right. You soon pass Rydal Mount, the home of William Wordsworth from 1813 to 1850. Immediately after passing Rydal Mount turn left onto an obvious trackway signposted as being a public bridleway to Grasmere. This is a very pleasant route that traverses the lower slopes of Nab Scar. Eventually, a little surprisingly, it becomes surfaced and gradually widens to become a roadway, soon after which it comes to a road junction. (1 $^1/_2$ miles)

4   Here turn right and follow the road downhill past Dove Cottage and across the main A591, where it becomes Stock Lane, into the village of Grasmere. ($^1/_2$ mile)

    (There are a number tea rooms in Grasmere but my own preference in fine weather is a small tea hut by the shoreline of the lake which has some pleasing views. It is situated a quarter of a mile from the church on the road described below in the following direction note.)

5   Walk a few yards past St Oswald's Church and turn left onto the road signposted as leading to the Information Centre. Follow the road for approximately half a mile till you locate a six bar gate on your left, over which is a fine uninterrupted view of the lake. Sited almost imperceptibly in the left-hand wall leading to the gate is a narrow gap giving access to a small flight of wooden steps and a sign indicating that it is the start of a permissive lake shore path. (1 mile)

6   Follow the path and on reaching the outflow of the lake, about forty yards before reaching the rather sturdy footbridge that spans it, follow a small path that veers off to the right. On reaching a small crest the path splits in two. Keep to the right-hand branch, the higher one, traversing along the lower slopes of Loughrigg above Rydal Water. This path reaches quite a spectacular 'cavern', the result of past quarrying, which is well worth some exploration. (1$^1/_2$ miles)

7   From the 'cavern' the path descends down to the left and becomes a trackway that upgrades to a surfaced roadway at a group of cottages. Within half a mile the road comes to a junction. ($^3/_4$ mile)

8   Here turn right. Follow the road for about a mile. After crossing a cattle grid on the left-hand side is a sturdy stone footbridge crossing over the river Rothay. Immediately on the other side of the bridge is the start of two paths. Both paths lead into Ambleside through the town park the right-hand path more directly. (1$^1/_2$ miles)

Walk 2 # THE TWO LANGDALES

Distance	8¹/₂ miles
Total feet of ascent	1000 feet
Suggested time	4 hours
Starting point	Elterwater (NY 328 048). Car park in the centre of the village.
Public transport	Bus. Ambleside to the Old Dungeon Ghyll Hotel. Service 516.

Because of the very nature of the Lake District there are few possible long level circular walks. This walk is about the longest there is of this type in the central Lakes, if you ignore the odd few undulations that make it less than perfectly flat. Almost the exact same circuit can be done by car, but then you would never be able to appreciate the full majesty of Great Langdale from a car as you can by walking, and indeed there are sections of this route, particularly in Little Langdale, that evoke the thought of just how wonderful the world must have been before the invention of the combustion engine.

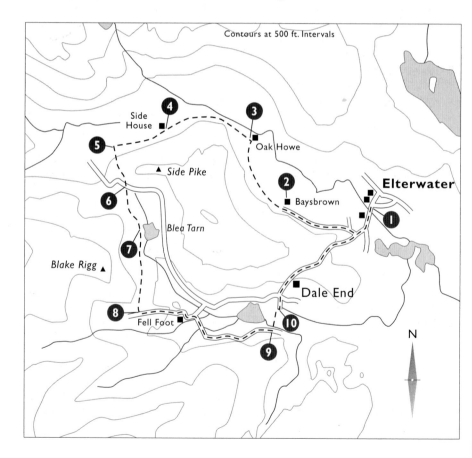

1   From the centre of the village follow the road signposted as leading to Coniston and Little Langdale. After passing the youth hostel take the first turn right. This narrow lane soon forks. Follow the right-hand surfaced branch indicated as being a cul de sac to Baysbrown Farm. (1¼ miles)

2   On reaching the farm the lane continues straight ahead as an unsurfaced trackway. A few hundred yards along this track another trackway branches off to the right; however this is not a right of way. It is the second trackway branching off to the right, a few more yards further on after a slight climb, which you should follow. A small sign indicates that this is a right of way. This trackway reduces to a footpath leading to Oak Howe. (³/₄ mile)

3   Immediately facing the barn at Oak Howe turn left onto what is initially a very grassy pathway. This is a distinct path and follows an undulating course to Side House Farm. Just before the entrance to the farm is a small footbridge. Do not cross over this bridge, but instead follow the rather faint path to the left, following the side of the beck over which the bridge crosses, uphill to a prominent wooden wall stile. (1 mile)

4   Once over this stile the path continues straight ahead. However, in places it is very indistinct and easy to lose. Two guiding points to look for are firstly another wall stile, and much further on, a five bar gate situated just above a group of conifer trees. From this five bar gate the path continues straight ahead to a second five bar gate in a stone wall. (³/₄ mile)

5   Here the path turns left following the wall, uphill to the crest of the gap between Side Pike and Blake Rigg, to a tall wooden stile. (¹/₄ mile)

6   Climb over the stile and cross straight over the roadway on the other side and along the wall opposite onto a piece of cobbled pathway which continues as a distinct path leading to the small wood on the western banks of Blea Tarn. (¹/₂ mile)

7   Entering the copse the path splits in two. Take the left-hand lower path. Emerging from the wood the path links up with a cobbled path. Here turn right. Within a few yards the cobbled path meets a kissing gate. From here the path continues downhill by a stream initially and then veers to the right, away from the stream, to link up with the Wrynose Pass road. (³/₄ mile)

8   Here turn left and follow the road downhill. Approximately a hundred yards after passing Fell Foot Farm at the bottom of the hill turn right off the road over an elegant little stone bridge onto a trackway. Passing over a second bridge, next to an isolated cottage, the track curves eastwards. Where it forks take the left-hand branch towards a group of cottages. About another hundred yards past the last cottage is a kissing gate in the wall to your left. (1¹/₂ miles)

9   From this gate a path leads down to Slater Bridge. Cross over the bridge and follow the path on the other side straight uphill to a farm access road ignoring the path branching to the right. (¹/₄ mile)

10 Here turn left. On reaching the road turn left and then immediately right onto another narrow lane indicated as being unsuitable for motor vehicles. Passing Dale End Farm the reason for the road's unsuitability for cars becomes evident, as here it becomes a rough unsurfaced trackway leading directly back to Elterwater. (1¹/₂ miles)

SILVER HOWE 1292 feet

Distance	4¹/₂ miles
Total feet of ascent	1200 feet
Suggested time	3 hours
Starting point	Grasmere (NY 336 075)

The visitor to Grasmere, looking about himself, or herself, for a modest fell to climb might well decide on Silver Howe, the most modest peak of all overlooking Grasmere; not a distinct peak, just a slight upturn on the skyline, but none the less a distinctive enough object to aim for. Once attained however it becomes immediately apparent that its right to be considered a summit, even a modest one, is totally unjustified; it is merely a promontory, a knobbled edge, of a very long broken ridge which separates the Vale of Grasmere from Langdale. Even so it is still a worthy walk that provides several pleasing views of Grasmere.

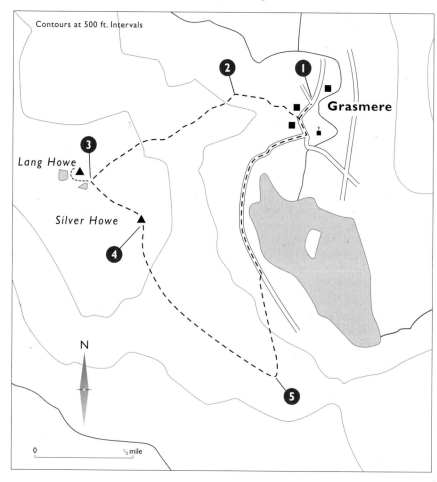

1   Starting from Sam Read's bookshop walk towards the Red Lion Hotel and take the first turning right just past the coffee shop onto a road signed 'No through road'. This soon takes on the appearance of a private driveway, and it does indeed lead to Allan Bank, once the former home of Wordsworth, but there is a public right of way along it. As the house comes into view the driveway branches in two. The right-hand branch is signposted as a 'Path', though it continues as a surfaced driveway to two attractive cottages. ($^1/_2$ mile)

2   Just before the cottages the drive branches in two, and the left-hand unsurfaced branch is signposted as leading to Silver Howe. Within a couple of yards after passing through a kissing gate this trackway reduces to a simple footpath. After a steepish climb of five hundred foot or so the gradient eases and the path begins following the side of a beck set in a deeply incised gully. At this point a path branches off to the left into the gully, climbing out of which it then heads directly to Silver Howe. But rather than take this option, keep to the path you are on to the right of the gully, which soon veers towards a rocky outcrop called Lang Howe, at the foot of which is a small tarn. As soon as this tarn becomes visible the path almost imperceptibly merges into another one. (1 mile)

3   This new path is the ridge path following the line, though obviously not the crest, of the ridge you will now almost have reached the top of. It is well worthwhile at this point to follow this ridge path uphill a few yards to the right, passing a second little tarnlet, and then scramble up to the top of Lang Howe from where there is an excellent view of the Langdale Pikes. This view may tempt you to follow the walk described on page 16 which follows the ridge further westwards onto Blea Rigg and then descends back to Grasmere via Easedale Tarn. The route in this walk, however, involves following the ridge path eastwards on to Silver Howe, which now appears to be a simple promontory of the ridge rather than a separate peak. ($^1/_4$ mile)

4   From Silver Howe the path continues along the ridge mostly downhill until the sharp hump of Dow Bank is reached. Crossing over this there is a slight saddle and then a second not so prominent 'hump'. At the foot of the second hump on the other side is a distinct path crossing from Elterwater to Grasmere. Directly ahead of you now, across the crest of the ridge, should be a line of conifer trees. If there is not then you have yet to reach the correct depression and should continue along the ridge further. ($1^1/_4$ miles)

5   On reaching what would seem to have been the old bridleway between Elterwater and Grasmere, though the map represents it as only being a footpath, turn left and follow it towards Grasmere. Within half a mile it joins the minor road that passes round the western side of Grasmere lake and provides the final section of this walk back to its starting point. ($1^1/_2$ miles)

Walk 4   # LOUGHRIGG 1099 feet.

Distance	6 miles
Total feet of ascent	1100 feet
Suggested time	3 hours
Starting point	Ambleside Market Cross (NY 376 046)

A close look at the 1:25,000 scale map of Loughrigg shows a myriad of little paths criss-crossing the top of the fell in every direction. It would probably take a year of daily ramblings to become completely familiar with every knoll and hummock of this complex little fell, though the path to the summit is straightforward enough. The summit of Loughrigg, at a little over one thousand feet, probably provides the best view in Lake District in relation to the effort involved. It affords a fine view of Langdale and the Langdale Pikes and another of the Vale of Grasmere, as well as being a good place to study the Fairfield Horseshoe. It is a good fell on which to encourage recalcitrant children to become fellwalkers, or for experienced walkers to grab an afternoon's ramble from a day of otherwise inhibiting rain.

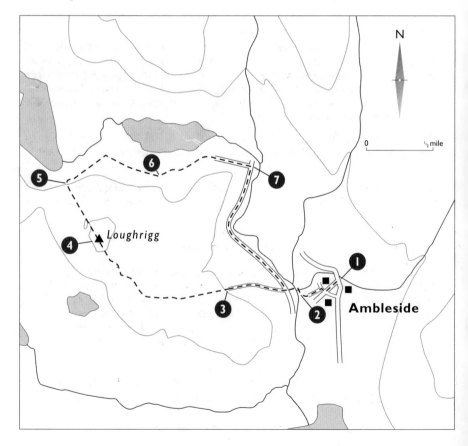

1   From the centre of Ambleside, from the Market Cross, walk towards The Climbers Shop and turn first left into Compston Road. After passing Zefferelli's cinema bear right, past the Walnut Fish Bar, into Vicarage Road, signposted as leading to Rothay Park and Loughrigg. Where the road terminates as a surfaced roadway it continues as a broad surfaced pathway across Rothay Park to a stone arched footbridge crossing over the Rothay river. ($^{1}/_{2}$ mile)

2   Cross over the bridge onto a roadway. Here turn right and follow the road sixty yards and turn left off the road onto a surfaced driveway. The driveway zigzags up the fellside providing an access to a number of houses. Ignore the footpath signposted to Clappersgate. After passing the last house, Pine Rigg, a large wooden building, the driveway, already now a rough track, reduces to a pathway. ($^{3}/_{4}$ mile)

3   The fell now becomes fairly open and undulating but the path is clear enough, though there is at least one false summit. The true summit is marked with a trig point. (1 mile)

4   Follow the path descending the fell on the other side of the trig point towards Grasmere. After a steep descent down an attractively cobbled section the path comes to a junction with another pathway just above a coppice of fir trees. ($^{1}/_{2}$ mile)

5   Here turn right and follow the path descending gently along the lower slopes of Loughrigg. Where the path reaches a wall there is a staggered intersection with another path. Instead of continuing downhill here turn right and follow the intersecting path traversing along the side of the fell above Rydal Water. This path soon reaches a quite spectacular 'cavern', the result of past quarrying, which is well worth exploring. (1 mile)

6   From the 'cavern' the path descends down to the left and becomes a trackway that upgrades to a surfaced roadway. Within a half mile the road comes to a junction. ($^{3}/_{4}$ mile)

7   Here turn right. Follow the road for about a mile. After crossing a cattle grid on the left-hand side is the stone footbridge you crossed earlier. From here retrace your earlier steps back into Ambleside. ($1^{1}/_{2}$ miles)

Literary Associations

One of the most informative guides to the Lake District published in recent years is Grevel Lindop's *Literary Guide to the Lake District*. Reference to it invariably puts a new perspective on most Lakeland walks. In the case of the walk described on these pages it reveals the road followed between Rydal and Ambleside has more than one house with literary connections: Loughrigg Holme was the home of Edward Quillinan the Irish sea captain who married William Wordsworth's daughter Dora; Fox Ghyll was the home of Thomas De Quincey between 1820 - 1825, and Fox How was the holiday home of Dr Thomas Arnold the headmaster of Rugby school and later his poet son Matthew. Wordsworth advised Arnold on the architecture of the building.

Walk 5   # WANSFELL 1581 feet.

Distance	6 miles
Total feet of ascent	1800 feet
Suggested time	4 hours
Starting point	Ambleside Market Cross (NY 376 046)

Wansfell is an extremely good panoramic viewpoint overlooking the town of Ambleside. It affords not only an excellent view of Ambleside but also a view of the whole length of Windermere and some impressive views of the Lakeland fells, and on a good day the peaks of the Yorkshire Dales. The walk is steep to begin with, but after the summit of Wansfell is attained it becomes an easy ramble, descending firstly down to the village of Troutbeck, probably the most attractive village in the Lake District and well worth a little exploration. The journey back to Ambleside is then along walled trackways and across undulating fields, mostly always with views of Windermere, and lastly through a half mile of woodland.

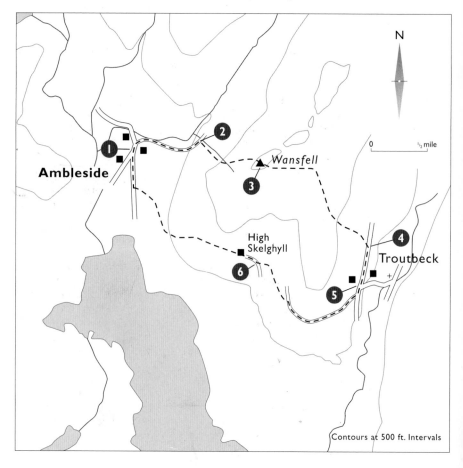

1   From the Market Cross walk southwards to Barclays Bank. Here turn left in to the lane, Stock Ghyll Lane, that runs between the bank and the Market Hall. The lane makes a sharp left hand turn at the back of the bank and starts climbing uphill. The road soon broadens out and becomes quite steep. On reaching an annex to Charlotte Mason's College however it narrows again and becomes a right of way only to walkers. A few hundred yards along this more level, narrow section of road on your right is to be located a stile. ($^3/_4$ mile)

2   The stile gives access to a path signposted as leading to Troutbeck via Wansfell. Climb over the stile and follow the path, which initially follows the side of a small stream, to the top of Wansfell. ($^3/_4$ mile)

3   The path continues over Wansfell descending eastwards towards the village of Troutbeck. It is a very distinct path and there is no problem following it. After descending nearly five hundred feet it reaches an enclosed trackway, Nanny Lane. Here turn right and follow the track downhill into the village of Troutbeck. ($1^3/_4$ miles)

4   On reaching the roadway turn right and follow the road as far as the village Post Office, situated on the ground floor of the village hall. ($^1/_2$ mile) (*If however you wish to discover the Mortal Man or the Queen's Head, or both, before discovering the Post Office, turn left, as both these hostelries are situated at the northern end of the village. The Post Office itself though serves tea and coffee.*)

5   Starting from the entrance of the village hall, at the gable end of the building, is the start of a signposted bridleway, Robin Lane, to Ambleside. Continue along this trackway. After walking three quarters of a mile along this enclosed trackway branch off to the left through a kissing gate next to a six bar gate onto another bridleway clearly signposted as leading to Ambleside. It leads firstly however to an access road leading to High Skelghyll Farm. ($1^1/_4$ miles)

6   Here turn right and follow the access road to the farm. Pass through the farmyard up to a six bar gate at the left-hand gable end of the farm house. This gives access to a well defined trackway which leads without difficulty back to Ambleside. ($1^1/_2$ miles)

A Quiet Pint

When Alfred Wainwright appeared on the radio programme Desert Island Discs almost his very first words were these: "Music has never played a great part in my life - in fact, more often than not I've found it an irritant." Music often is when chosen by someone else. Unfortunately most publicans now seem unaware of this fact and many pubs that could be congenial are made unpleasant with the introduction of electronically produced music. The Ambleside area, however, does quite well for pubs that are music free. The Britannia in Elterwater, The Three Shires in Little Langdale, the O.D.G. in Great Langdale (see page 23) and The Drunken Dunk near Hawkshead all have bars that are free of piped music. But pride of place as a music free pub must go to The Golden Rule in Ambleside: not only does it eschew piped music it also eschews serving hot food. It is how all pubs once used to be, save in one respect - it is connected to the internet.

BLEA RIGG

Distance	7 miles
Total feet of ascent	1800 feet
Suggested time	4 hours
Starting point	Grasmere (NY 336 075)

Blea Rigg is not a peak, not even a minor peak, even though Wainwright devotes a chapter to it in his volume on the central fells; it is simply the last part of a long broken ridge separating Langdale from Easedale. It is however a fine and interesting ridge to walk along having several knolls and crags worthy of investigation and a number of pleasing little tarns to admire. It also offers some splendid views of Langdale, especially the Langdale Pikes. It is therefore a satisfying walk in itself, especially when descending via Easedale Tarn, even though there is no actual 'conquest' of a summit involved. Even so having obtained the almost two thousand feet of ascent which this walk involves, and being so close to an actual summit, users of this guide may wish to forge ahead on to High White Stones, unless it is shrouded in mist. Between directional notes 4 and 5, therefore, I've given some consideration to this possibility.

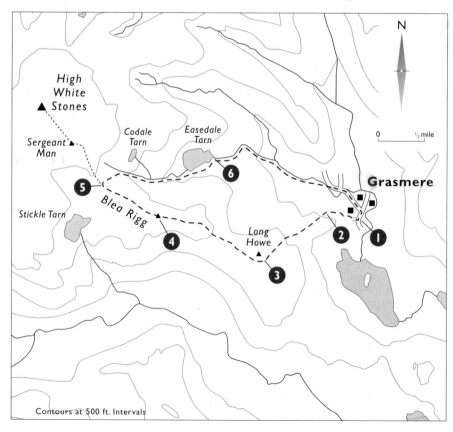

1   Starting from Sam Read's bookshop walk towards the Red Lion Hotel and take the first turning right just past the coffee shop onto a road signed 'No through road'. This soon takes on the appearance of a private driveway, and it does indeed lead to Allan Bank once the former home of Wordsworth, there is, however, a public right of way along it. As the house comes into view the driveway branches in two. The right-hand branch is signposted as being a 'Path', though it continues as a surfaced driveway to two attractive cottages. (½ mile)

2   Just before the cottages the drive branches in two. Take the left-hand unsurfaced branch, signposted as leading to Silver Howe. Within a couple of yards after passing through a kissing gate this trackway reduces to a simple footpath. After a steepish climb of five hundred foot or so the gradient eases and the sprawling nature of the fell becomes apparent. Making sure not to follow a path branching off to the left, the path you began on continues towards a rocky outcrop called Lang Howe, at the foot of which is a small tarn. As soon as this tarn becomes visible the path almost imperceptibly merges into another path. (1 mile)

3   This new path is the ridge path following the line, though obviously not at this point the crest, of the ridge you will now almost have reached the top of. Here turn right to follow the ridge westwards. It is a very broken ridge and has two distinct rises in it. The second rise is a distinct conglomeration of solid rock outcrops. This is Blea Rigg itself. It is as you begin to ascend Blea Rigg that looking down to your right, for the first time, you should see Easedale Tarn. There is no distinct top to Blea Rigg - the ridge simply levels out. (1¼ miles)

4   After a few hundred yards of walking along the ensuing section of ridge away to your right you should gain a clear view of Codale Tarn. Shortly after this to your left you should obtain a view of Stickle Tarn below the precipitous face of Pavey Ark. It is after you obtain this view of Stickle Tarn you should begin looking for the start of a path descending towards Codale. This comes within the next few hundred yards. The start of the path is distinguished by a series of small cairns little more than ten yards apart from one another. (¾ mile)

(At this point should you be imbued with the idea of obtaining 'higher things' you may wish to consider that by continuing less than another half mile further along the ridge path and climbing only another five hundred feet you can reach the top of Sergeant Mann 2,414 feet. Beyond that, less than half a mile and almost a level walk away, is High White Stones at 2,500 feet. This excursion into 'peak bagging', including both peaks, should add less than an hour to the walk but will doubtless give you a greater sense of achievement. The descent from either peak via Easedale Tarn is best followed on page 28 from directional note 6 onwards. Alternatively the descent can be made by reversing the walk on page 28 as far as directional note 4, and then descending down Far Easedale. If however you feel you've climbed enough for one day....)

5   Turn right and follow the path downhill. The path actually bypasses Codale Tarn and descends down to Easedale Tarn. (1¼ miles)

6   From Easedale Tarn the path follows the side of the tarn's outflow, soon forming the short waterfall of Sour Milk Gill, into Easedale valley. Following the valley floor the path eventually meets up with Easedale Road which leads directly back into Grasmere. (2 miles)

LINGMOOR 1530 feet.

Distance	7 ¹/₂ miles
Total feet of ascent	1600 feet
Suggested time	4 hours
Starting point	Elterwater (NY 328 048). Car park in the centre of the village.
Public transport	Bus. Ambleside to the Old Dungeon Ghyll Hotel. Service 516.

Until I came to write this guide I had never actually visited Lingmoor as it does not easily link in with any of its taller neighbours - and perhaps more significantly it just doesn't look that interesting from the valley. From Elterwater it looks a long unshapely lump. But taking advice from a Mr. Trevor Wright, who then worked in the Information Centre at Water Head near Ambleside, as to which was the best route to take I discovered Lingmoor is actually a delightful fell, full of variety and surprises, including its own intriguing, slightly mystical, tarn. It was no surprise to me to find, therefore, out of a set of twelve postcards of the Lake District which were published shortly after I made this discovery two of the views were taken from Lingmoor.

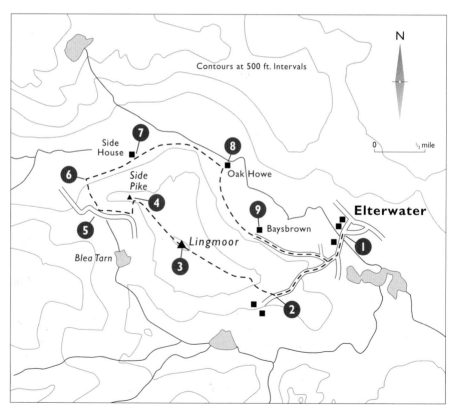

1   From the centre of the village follow the road signposted as leading to Coniston and Little Langdale. Take the first turn right. This narrow lane soon forks. Follow the left-hand unsurfaced branch. This rough trackway climbs steeply uphill and then becomes quite level and open. The track leads to a small group of farms. About a hundred yards from the point at which these buildings first become visible on your right is the start of a pathway leading up the fellside beginning from a six bar gate next to which is a narrower gate. (1 mile)

2   This is a very pleasing constructed pathway that zigzags its way up the fellside. Nearing the top the path branches in two and it is the right-hand branch you should take. The path soon comes to a very splendid and sturdy dry stone wall built along the crest of the fell. The path now parallels the wall following its undulating course to the summit of Lingmoor, though just before reaching the summit the wall is superseded by a very unimpressive wire fence. (1 ¼ miles)

3   From the summit continue to follow the wire fence which continues along the crest of the fell following the remains of a ruined wall. Where this fence takes a sharp turn left it soon terminates however as at this point the wall has been restored. Although the wall initially seems to be leading sharply downhill to Blea Tarn it soon curves back round to follow the crest of the ridge downhill to the base of the cliff face of Side Pike. (³/₄ mile)

4   From the lowest point of the saddle between Lingmoor and Side Pike, leading away to the left at right angles from the wall is a wire fence. Follow this downhill. A hundred yards from the roadway a simple wooden stile crosses the fence giving access to a narrow path veering off to the right round the base of Side Pike to the top of the gap over which the road passes. (¹/₂ mile)

    (At this point my own preference would be to return to Elterwater via Little Langdale, but as this route is described on page 4 in the Two Langdales Walk from directional note 6 onwards, below is described the return route via Great Langdale which is a mile and a half shorter.)

5   From the top of the gap follow the path next to the parallel stone wall and fence leading downhill towards a copse of conifer trees. (¹/₄ mile)

6   On reaching the wire fence which encloses the copse of trees turn right and follow the path following the line of the fence north eastwards. After passing the conifer trees the path is none too obvious but keep walking directly ahead. Soon you should see the top of a wooden wall stile crossing the stone wall some hundred yards ahead. In heading for this you should find the path becomes clearer. Crossing over the stile the path heads for a second stile just above Side House Farm. From this second stile the path leads down to a small footbridge directly behind the farm. (³/₄ mile)

7   Do not cross over this footbridge into the farm but follow the path leading eastwards from the footbridge. This soon begins climbing uphill but only for a short distance and then takes a more level course to Oak Howe. (1 mile)

8   At Oak Howe keep to the right of the outer barn. The path continues at right angles to the barn passing to the right of the yew tree opposite, and then curves round to the south east eventually joining a trackway leading to Baysbrown Farm. (³/₄ mile)

9   From the farm the trackway continues as a surfaced driveway that leads back to the start of this walk and to Elterwater. (1¹/₂ miles)

Walk 8

HELM CRAG 1299 feet
& FAR EASEDALE

Distance	7 miles
Total feet of ascent	1800 feet
Suggested time	4¼ hours
Starting point	Grasmere (NY 336 075)

This walk is a shorter version of the High White Stones walk on page 28, involving an earlier descent down Far Easedale valley. Helm Crag is often known as the peak with the 'lion and the lamb' because of the shape of its summit crags. Once having reached the top of Helm Crag it would be a waste of effort simply to return straight back down again, so this walk continues along the ridge of which Helm Crag is the termination, although this involves another eight hundred feet of climbing. But then this also allows for a descent back to Grasmere along the length of Far Easedale. This valley can have changed very little since Wordsworth's day. Graced with several delightful small waterfalls it seems a whole world away from the tourist bustle of Grasmere. It is exceptionally peaceful and provides a good conclusion to a reasonably energetic walk.

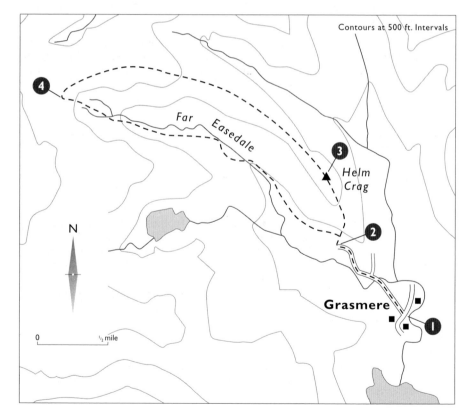

20

1   From Sam Read's bookshop in the centre of Grasmere walk north westwards along Easedale Road which is directly opposite the bookshop. Ignore the turning to the right, about half a mile along, signposted as leading to a youth hostel. Keep going straight ahead. After crossing an open field the road comes to a group of houses where it terminates. (1 mile)

2   Three trackways continue from the road's termination point. Only the right-hand track is a right of way and is signposted as leading to Helm Crag. This track soon splits in two. Again take the right-hand branch, which has a wooden signpost indicating that it leads to Helm Crag. It soon reduces to a pathway, and after a few hundred feet of ascent this also divides. This time take the left-hand slightly broader option and ignore the path following the wall to the right. There is no problem now following this very distinct path to the top of Helm Crag. The actual summit is a rocky outcrop, 'the Lion', to reach the top of which necessitates some scrambling that is perhaps best avoided. (^{1}/$_2$ mile)

3   The path continues north-westwards from the top of Helm Crag along a very broken and undulating ridge. At the far end the ridge becomes very broad and soggy and loses much of its definition as a ridge. The path though is quite clear and eventually reaches the remains of a former metal fence. A few hundred yards along the line of this former fence the path intersects with a bridleway which connects Grasmere with Borrowdale and is part of Wainwright's famed 'Coast to Coast route'. (2^1/$_4$ miles)

4   Here turn left onto the path leading down into Far Easedale. The path is very distinctive and there is no problem following it down the length of this quiet little valley. Towards the end of the valley it becomes more of a trackway veering a little away from the beck and linking back on to the first section of the walk which you should have no difficulty retracing back to Grasmere. (3^1/$_4$ miles)

De Quincey on Easedale

In an essay entitled *Reflections on Grasmere* which appeared in Tait's Edinburgh Magazine in 1839 Thomas De Quincey wrote this on Easedale:-

I have often thought, whilst looking with silent admiration upon this exquisite composition of landscape, with its miniature fields, running up like forest glades into miniature woods; its little columns of smoke, breathing up like incense to the household gods, from the hearths of two or three picturesque cottages - abodes of simple primitive manners, and what, from personal knowledge, I will call humble virtue - whilst my eyes rested on this charming combination of lawns and shrubberies I have thought that, if a scene on this earth could deserve to be sealed up, like the valley of Rasselas, against the intrusions of the world - if there were one to which a man would willingly surrender himself a prisoner for the years of a long life - this it is - this Easedale - which would justify the choice and recompense the sacrifice.

NB Rasselas was the name of a fictional Abyssinian prince ordained never to leave a valley of great beauty and serenity who appears in a novel by Samuel Johnson published in 1759.

Walk 9   # PIKE O' BLISCO 2304 feet

Distance	4 miles
Total feet of ascent	2000 feet
Suggested time	3$^{1}/_{2}$ hours
Starting point	Old Dungeon Ghyll Hotel (NY 286 061)
	Car park next to hotel.
Public transport	Bus. Ambleside to the Old Dungeon Ghyll Hotel
	Service 516.

Pike o' Blisco is one of the few conical shaped peaks in the Lake District. It is also very rocky and rugged, giving it the feel of a 'real' mountain and the walker who reaches the top of it a real sense of achievement. Yet Pike o' Blisco is really only a modest fell as far as height goes, being almost a thousand feet lower than Scafell Pike, England's highest. So this is a good fell for the novice fellwalker to start on as it really requires only a modest degree of effort. For the very energetic Pike o' Blisco can be fitted into a circuit including Crinkle Crags and Bowfell by following direction note 4 onwards on page 31 when reaching directional note 4 in this walk.

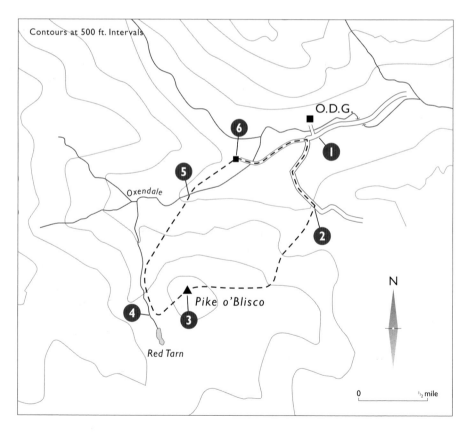

22

1   From the Old Dungeon Ghyll Hotel walk back to the main road and turn right. Follow the road as it turns left to make its ascent over to Little Langdale. Crossing over a cattle grid the road begins pulling uphill. At the corner of the second sharp hairpin bend a distinct path leads off to the right. ($\frac{1}{2}$ mile)

2   This is a distinct path and there is no problem following it to the top of Pike o' Blisco. There are two cairns on the summit, of which the furthest as you approach seems to be the highest. ($1\frac{1}{4}$ miles)

3   From the summit a distinct path descends 600 feet to the southwest towards Red Tarn. The path does not actually lead to the tarn itself but to a point along the tarn's outflow a few hundred feet north of the tarn. ($\frac{1}{4}$ mile)

4   Here the path crosses over the beck and continues uphill to Crinkle Crags. But note just before crossing the beck another path leads away to the right back down to Langdale. As modest as this path looks to begin with it soon becomes very rocky and eroded and a long difficult descent seems in prospect. But after a short distance the path becomes almost level as it traverses away to the right. After a few hundred yards however it commences a long, steep descent which was once every bit as difficult and awkward as the earlier part of the descent suggested it would be but now is no longer so, thanks to the construction of a long twisting cobbled pathway that has made the descent infinitely easier. At the foot of the descent the path comes to a single-beamed footbridge crossing Oxendale Beck. (1 mile)

5   Cross over the bridge and turn right and follow the very broad path to Stool End Farm. There is no need to climb over the prominent stile on the way; simply keep to the path going to the right of the wall. The stile is there simply to cause unnecessary torment to aching limbs. ($\frac{1}{2}$ mile)

6   From the farm follow the obvious farm access road back to the Old Dungeon Ghyll Hotel. ($\frac{1}{2}$ mile)

O.D.G.

The public bar of the Old Dungeon Ghyll Hotel, the O.D.G. as it is mostly known, is without much doubt the most spartan bar in the Lake District, being, after all, a former cattle byre. The bar is very popular with rock climbers as rising above the hotel are several major rock climbing crags. Gracing the wall of the bar is a large picture entitled: "A Climber in Paradise", which features a climber enjoying heavenly, bacchanalian revelry. The subject of the painting is a climber called Jack Thornton, who was barman of the O.D.G. at the time the picture was painted in the 1950's. Jack Thornton was also a founder member of the Langdale Mountain Rescue Team. The artist was a student of the Royal College of Art who herself features in the top right-hand corner of the painting lying recumbent outside her tent. Boisterous as the bar is at times it can also be very peaceful as it is totally free of piped music.

Walk 10   # RED SCREES 2493 feet

Distance	7¹/₂ miles
Total feet of ascent	2300 feet
Suggested time	5 hours
Starting point	Ambleside Market Cross (NY 376 046)

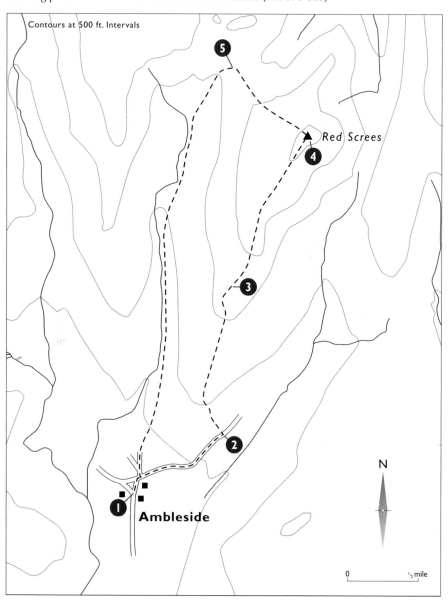

Contours at 500 ft. Intervals

Red Screes

N

Ambleside

0   ¹/₂ mile

Red Screes doesn't easily link up with any of its neighbouring hills. For this reason it is relatively less frequented than they are, and the majority of people who do ascend Red Screes probably do so from the top of Kirkstone Pass, taking advantage of the fifteen hundred foot start this gives them. All this leads to the ridge from Ambleside to the top of Red Screes being comparatively quiet compared to all the other fells around. This is a delightful rambling fell to ascend and a good introduction to high level fellwalking. The return route via Scandale is along a remarkably long enclosed trackway. All over these hills to the north of Ambleside are extensive lines of dry stone walls. Some specific reason obviously accounts for it though I've yet to discover it. This walk gives a good appreciation of those past labours.

1   From the Market Cross walk up North Road. At the road junction turn right onto Smithy Brow, not that is onto Fairview Road. Smithy Brow is the start of a long steep road up to Kirkstone Pass. You have almost a mile to walk up this road before you reach the start of the path leading onto the fell, beginning from the left hand side of the road. Be sure to ignore the first footpath you come to on your left, indicated with an arrow on a slate sign just before Rowanfield Guest House. This simply leads back into Ambleside! The start of the Red Screes path is a further quarter of a mile uphill, a small gate with a wooden signpost next to it. (1 mile)

2   Passing through this gate the path leads uphill between two roughly parallel walls forming a broad path along which sheep were originally driven off the fell. However, seemingly later on the fell was divided into a number of large fields, causing the former drove path to cease to have any purpose. So whilst the right-hand wall has been maintained as a boundary wall the left-hand wall has fallen into disrepair, and in some sections has all but disappeared. However the right of way continues to follow this former drove path, tending mostly to follow the right-hand wall, and crossing over a number of wooden stiles where the newer walls have cut across it. The route leads onto and then follows the crest of the ridge. But after diverting slightly from the crest, to round a more steeper section, the original intake walls broaden out to enclose the fell. (1 mile)

3   Here the path makes its own course onto the crest of the ridge and onto the summit of Red Screes, marked with a trig point next to a surprising summit tarn. ($1^1/_4$ miles)

4   From the summit, head in a north-westerly direction to Scandale Pass. Despite its representation on the O.S. map there is no real path. So from the summit as you descend keep veering to the left, crossing firstly over a ruined wall contouring round the fell and then moving towards a less ruinous wall running downhill. Next to this wall is a small path leading down to the head of Scandale Pass. ($^3/_4$ mile)

5   At the lowest point of the pass a more distinct path cuts across. Here turn left and follow the new path down into the valley. The path eventually becomes an enclosed trackway leading directly back into Ambleside. ($3^1/_2$ miles)

THE LANGDALE PIKES

Distance	7 miles
Total feet of ascent	2500 feet
Suggested time	5 hours
Starting point	New Dungeon Ghyll Hotel (NY 296 064)
	Car park adjacent to roadway.
Public transport	Bus. Ambleside to the Old Dungeon Ghyll Hotel
	Service 516.

From the New Dungeon Ghyll Hotel the Langdale Pikes must offer one of the most challenging sights in the Lake District; a half dozen miniature peaks and summits seem to crowd in on top of one another. It is compelling to want to go and climb them all. At Stickle Tarn you should easily make out the diagonal line of Jack's Rake moving from right to left up across the cliff face of Pavey Ark. This is one of the routes to the top of Pavey Ark. The route taken in this walk however is less likely to cause a cardiac arrest. After Pike o' Stickle which provides a splendid 'perch' from which to look down into Langdale, the route descends via Stake Pass which provides a gentler gradient compared to that of the ascent and will invariably be much quieter.

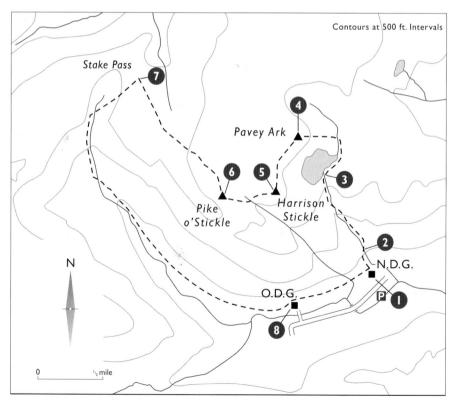

1   Walk up the driveway past the New Dungeon Ghyll Hotel to the gateway by the gable end of Stickle Cottage. Starting from the gate are two pathways. Take the left-hand path. This soon splits in two. Take the right-hand branch running besides a wire fence. This cobbled path soon crosses over Stickle Ghyll by way of broad footbridge and follows the right-hand side of the beck. ($^1/_4$ mile)

2   There follows a steep ascent up along the side of the beck. A few hundred feet above the footbridge what seems to be the main line of the path crosses back over to the left-hand side of the beck, though there is an alternative path that keeps to the right-hand side, which would obviously be best to keep to if the beck were in spate. Either route leads to the outflow of Stickle Tarn. ($^1/_2$ mile)

3   From the outflow of the tarn follow the path moving round the eastern edge of the tarn, to your right as you look at the tarn, to where it meets a beck flowing into it. Here the path follows the beck upstream a short distance then crosses over the beck and ascends the eastern slopes of Pavey Ark to its summit. ($^3/_4$ mile)

4   From the top of Pavey Ark a distinct path curves around the tops of the fells overlooking Stickle Tarn onto Harrison Stickle. Even though the ground is very rocky and broken there is no difficulty following it. ($^1/_2$ mile)

5   From the top of Harrison Stickle a path leads directly westwards to Pike o' Stickle, a mound shaped peak reminiscent on a grand scale of the proverbial sore thumb, firstly dipping down to and then climbing up from the head waters of Dungeon Ghyll. It is very soggy in parts. ($^1/_2$ mile)

6   Leading away to the north from Pike o' Stickle, to your right as you approach from Harrison Stickle, is a path leading to Stake Pass, best described as following the highest piece of land leading away from the Pike. There are actually two paths to begin with. It is the broader left-hand path you should take. This crosses over some rather featureless soggy terrain until you come to some small rounded hummocks which are glacial moraines. Snaking through these humps is a more defined path - an old packhorse route crossing from Borrowdale to Langdale. (1 mile)

7   Here turn left and follow the old packhorse route down into Langdale. At the foot of the pass is a broad path leading to the Old Dungeon Ghyll Hotel. ($2^3/_4$ miles)

8   Just as you reach a five bar gate and kissing gate leading to the hotel follow the wall leading from these gates fifty yards uphill to another five bar gate and kissing gate. Through these higher gates a path leads back to the New Dungeon Ghyll. This path however is a little undulating so if you are weary despite the traffic you may prefer to use the main road to get back to the New Dungeon Ghyll Hotel as it is decidedly flatter. ($^3/_4$ mile)

Walk 12 **HIGH WHITE STONES 2500 feet**

Distance	9 ½ miles
Total feet of ascent	2700 feet
Suggested time	6 hours
Starting point	Grasmere (NY 336 075)

High White Stones, the highest point on this walk, is one of the flattest tops in the Lakeland, however it is one of Lakeland's best viewpoints as it is roughly the most central fell in the Lake District. In each direction are extensive views of other fells. Perhaps more than half the fell tops above two thousand feet can be seen from this point. If the summit is flat however both the ascent to it and the descent from it are far more varied, particularly the descent which passes Easedale tarn, Codale tarn and a series of waterfalls.

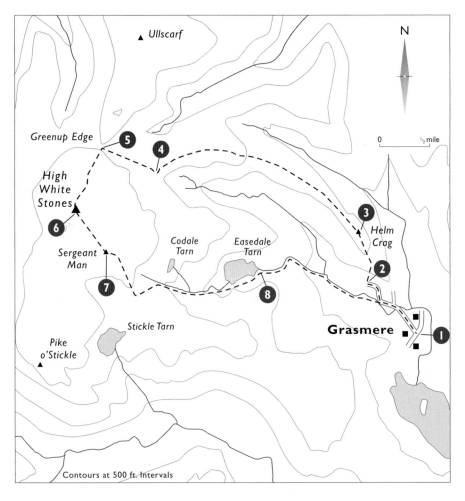

1   From Sam Read's bookshop in the centre of Grasmere walk north westward along Easedale Road the start of which is directly opposite the bookshop. Ignore the turning to the right, about half a mile along, sign posted as leading to a youth hostel and keep going straight ahead. After crossing an open field the road comes to a group of houses where it terminates. (1 mile)

2   Three trackways continue from the road's termination point. Only the right-hand track is a right of way and is sign posted as leading to Helm Crag. This track soon splits in two. Again take the right-hand branch, which has a wooden signpost indicating that it leads to Helm Crag. It soon reduces to a pathway, and after a few hundred feet of ascent this too splits in two. This time take the left-hand slightly broader option and ignore the path following the wall to the right. There is no problem now following this very distinct path to the top of Helm Crag. The actual summit is a rocky outcrop, 'the Lion', to reach the top of which necessitates some scrambling, which is perhaps best avoided. ($^1/_2$ mile)

3   The path continues north westwards from the top of Helm Crag along a very broken and undulating ridge. At its far end the ridge becomes very broad and soggy and loses much of its definition as a ridge. The path along it though is quite clear and eventually reaches the remains of a former metal fence. A few hundred yards along the line of this former fence the path intersects with a bridleway which connects Grasmere with Borrowdale via Greenup Edge and is part of Wainwright's famed 'Coast to Coast route'. ($2^1/_4$ miles)

4   At this point turn right and follow the former packhorse route uphill to Greenup Edge, the shallow col between Ullscarf and High White Stones. The top of this is distinguished by the remains of another former metal fence. ($^3/_4$ mile)

5   Here turn left and follow the path following the line of the former fence towards the top of High White Stones. On reaching more level ground the path veers away from the line of the fence to the top of High White Stones itself marked with a trig point. ($^3/_4$ mile)

6   From the top of High White Stones a distinct path heads roughly southwards to Pike o' Stickle, the prominent mound shaped peak which sticks out like a sore thumb. Veering off to the left from the start of this path, in a south-easterly direction, towards some metal fence posts is another less distinct path. This is the path you should follow. After a few hundred yards you should find that the path approaches another less prominent mound-shaped top, Sergeant Man. ($^1/_2$ mile)

7   Follow the path that leads round to the east of Sergeant Man, to the left as you approach it from High White Stones. This soon leads on to a very broken ridge called Blea Rigg which separates the corries containing Stickle Tarn and Easedale Tarn. Shortly after Easedale Tarn comes into view on your left, the path divides. Take the left branch. Soon after Codale Tarn becomes apparent the path divides again. Again take the left branch which descends to Easedale Tarn. ($1^3/_4$ miles)

8   From Easedale Tarn the path follows the side of the tarn's outflow, which soon forms the short waterfall of Sour Milk Gill, into Easedale valley. Following the valley floor the path eventually meets up with Easedale Road where the walk started. Here turn right and follow the road back into Grasmere. (2 miles)

Walk 13   # CRINKLE CRAGS 2816 feet & BOWFELL 2960 feet

Distance	8¹/₂ miles
Total feet of ascent	3500 feet
Suggested time	6¹/₂ hours
Starting point	Old Dungeon Ghyll Hotel (NY 286 061) Car park next to hotel.
Public transport	Bus. Ambleside to the Old Dungeon Ghyll Hotel Service 516.

This is one of the classic fell walks of Lakeland - around the skyline of the head of Langdale. Called Crinkle Crags because of the crinkly nature of its skyline, the path crossing its crest has many twists and turns revealing several surprises. Bowfell by contrast is less complicated. The lines of the fell sweep up to a distinctive graceful peak from which the whole of Langdale can be surveyed. The descent route from Bowfell back to Langdale chosen in this walk uses a lesser known route that links in to the old packhorse route over Stake Pass, and thus avoids the steeper and more populous descent down Rossett Gill.

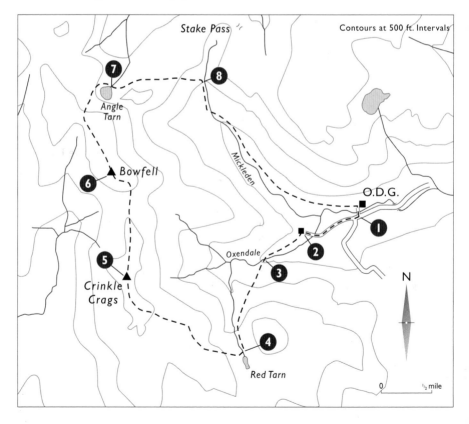

1   Exit from the Old Dungeon Ghyll Hotel car park and turn right. The road soon turns sharp left but straight ahead next to a red letter box is a six bar farm gate. Continue through this gate along a surfaced access road to Stool End Farm. ($\frac{1}{2}$ mile)

2   Pass through the farmyard and through a gateway to the left of the farmhouse onto a very obvious pathway. Ignore the right-hand branch of this path climbing uphill along the very steep prominent ridge known as the Band, but keep to the left-hand branch following the wall leading into Oxendale. Walk a short way along the valley, through a sheep fold, to a narrow single beam footbridge crossing over Oxendale Beck. ($\frac{1}{2}$ mile)

3   Cross over the footbridge and continue along the path on the other side which soon begins making a steep ascent up to Red Tarn. Just before reaching Red Tarn, before it comes properly into view, where the ground levels, the path comes to a 'T' junction with another path, next to Brown Gill. (1 mile)

4   Here turn right and cross over Brown Gill and continue on the path climbing between Great Knott and Cold Pike onto Crinkle Crags. Between the first 'crinkle' and the second there is a distinct gap from which the path ascends a small gully to reach the summit of the fell. This route involves a small climb of about seven foot known as 'Bad Step'. This is not difficult but can be avoided if necessary by moving left from the base of the gully and taking a curved route of ascent to the top. ($1\frac{1}{2}$ miles)

5   From the highest point on Crinkle Crags move northwards along the ridge descending to 'Three Tarns', from which a very visible path climbs to the summit of Bowfell. (1 mile)

6   From the summit of Bowfell a path descends northwards via Ore Gap to Angle Tarn. As you descend down to Angle Tarn, note a path leading away from the outflow of the tarn north-eastwards to Stake Pass. (1 mile)

7   From Angle Tarn take the path described above leading to Stake Pass. A hundred yards from the tarn another path veers off to the right towards a distinctive boulder. This path is so indistinct to begin with you may doubt its validity, but after a hundred yards or so it becomes more evident. It leads to a small gap between Rossett Crag and Black Crags overlooking Mickleden, from which a delicate cairned path descends diagonally down to the left a few hundred feet, to meet up with the former packhorse route leading down from Stake Pass. (1 mile)

8   Follow the old packhorse route down in to Mickleden and along the valley floor back to the Old Dungeon Ghyll Hotel. (2 miles)

Walk 14 **THE FAIRFIELD HORSESHOE**

Highest point	2863 feet
Distance	10½ miles
Total feet of ascent	3150 feet
Suggested time	6½ hours
Starting point	Ambleside Market Cross (NY 376 046)

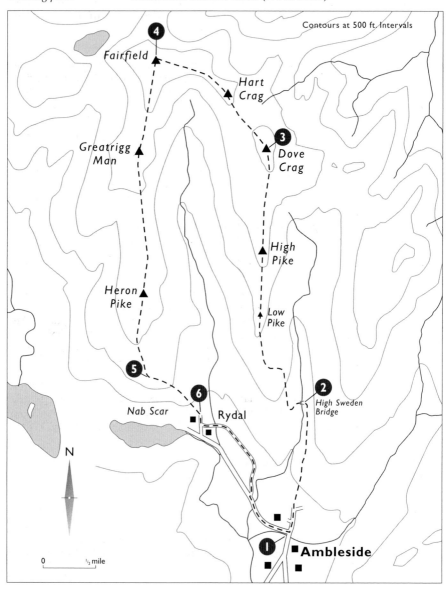

Exploring the streets of Ambleside the visitor will often glimpse a group of impressive and inviting hills lying to the north of the town. These are the hills which form the Fairfield Horseshoe, one of Lakeland's classic high level walks. It is a surprisingly long walk, for Fairfield looks much closer to Ambleside than it actually is, and the undulations involved can be taxing. The top of Fairfield is a delightful place to be on a fine day. Its name has always seemed very appropriate to me as the top is very broad and flat like a field and is actually quite fair looking as the rock on the summit is whitish in colour. My reference book however tells me that in this case the 'field' part of the name is a corruption of 'fell', and the name therefore simply means pleasant mountain.

1   From the Market Cross walk up North Road, passing the Unicorn Inn on your left, to a road junction. At the junction turn right and walk uphill. Take the first turn left into Sweden Bridge Lane. Belle Vue Lane soon branches off to the left. Ignore this turning and continue uphill. After a hundred yards there is a fork in the road, bear left here along the continuation of Sweden Bridge Lane. Soon this becomes a very attractive enclosed trackway leading, not surprisingly, to High Sweden Bridge. (1½ miles)

2   Cross over the bridge, pass through a small gate and turn left. The path climbs uphill and joins up with a more substantial path cum trackway. Follow this route northwards. After a short distance it reaches the crest of the ridge along which runs perhaps the most impressive dry stone wall in the Lake District. Continue along the path running alongside the wall, over Low Pike and High Pike and on to Dove Crag, spot height 2,603 feet. (2¾ miles)

3   From here the path turns north westwards along the ridge over Hart Crag and on to Fairfield itself. (1½ miles)

    (The summit of Fairfield is quite flat, so to enjoy the best views possible spend some time exploring the northern and north-eastern perimeters of the fell top from which some impressive views are obtainable. Because of its flat nature and plethora of cairns the summit of Fairfield is also a splendid place for getting lost if the weather is bad. If you are in mist therefore it is best to take a compass bearing. Otherwise you may find yourself following the wrong line of cairns and ending up in Patterdale or Grasmere.)

4   From the circular shelter situated on what seems to be the very top of Fairfield turn south towards Greatrigg Man. You should soon pick up a well cairned path. This follows the crest of a very distinct ridge over Greatrigg Man on to Heron Pike and eventually on to the top of Nab Scar overlooking Rydal Water. (3 miles)

5   The following descent down to the hamlet of Rydal is quite steep, but has been made easier due to the work which was done on the path some years ago. (½ mile)

6   Once reaching the roadway walk downhill and after passing Rydal Mount, the former home of Wordsworth, take the first turn left along an unsurfaced access road leading behind the imposing looking Rydal Hall. Surprisingly this is a public right of way that continues through the parkland of the Hall to the main road back to Ambleside. (1½ miles)

Walk 15   # STANAH TO GRASMERE VIA HELVELLYN 3113 feet

Starting point	Stanah (NY 318 189)
Return point	Grasmere (NY 336 075)
Distance	9 miles
Total feet of ascent	3100 feet
Suggested time	6 hours
Public transport	Bus. Lancaster to Keswick. Service 555/6.

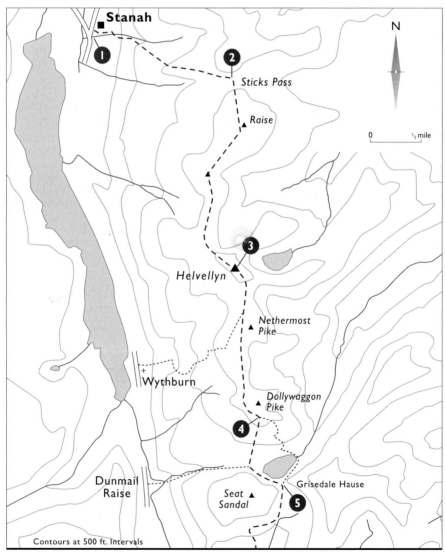

This is a linear walk from north to south along the crest of the Helvellyn range which probably gives the walker a better appreciation of the mountain, the third highest in England, than do the more usual circular walks. The walk's feasibility is made possible by the 555/6 bus route that gives ready access to the start of the walk from either Ambleside or Grasmere.

Alight from the Lancaster to Keswick bus at Stanah at the junction of the A591 and the B5322.

1 Follow the B5322 northwards about 40 yards and take the first turn right, next to the village hall, along a access road. This soon forks. Take the left branch. Where this branch takes a sharp left continue straight ahead to a steep wall stile which gives access to a path signposted as leading to Sticks Pass. Crossing over this stile the path climbs up to a second stile next to what appears to be a small bridge - but look closer. A short climb further up the path comes to a gate. Pass through this gate and turn right over a footbridge. You will soon see a sign pointing to a path veering off to the right towards Grasmere. Ignore this path. Your path is the more worn path straight ahead, next to Stanah Gill. This path is very steep to begin with but the gradient slackens after about 1500 feet. It takes an interesting line of ascent to the top of Sticks Pass, crossing over to the next little valley to do so. (1³/₄ miles)

2 At the top of Sticks Pass turn right and follow the crest of the ridge. This involves pulling up to the summit of Raise where the ridge becomes fairly level for about a mile crossing over White Side, after which there is a final steep climb of a few hundred feet to the top of Helvellyn. (2 miles)

3 From the summit walk south along a very distinct ridge path. Half a mile from the summit another path branches off to the right which descends down to Wythburn. Make sure to ignore this and keep to the higher path. Better views still are obtainable by ignoring the path altogether and walking along the actual edge of the ridge and rejoining the path between Nethermost Pike and Dollywaggon Pike. Do not do so in icy conditions, however, unless you are fully equipped. Follow the main path as far as a single isolated sturdy metal post that stands by the side of the path directly in line with the top of Dollywaggon. (1¹/₂ miles)

4 This post once supported a gate as here was once a fence that ran along the former county boundary between Cumberland and Westmorland. Follow the remains of the line of this fence directly downhill. In the lower part of the descent the line continues as a very ruinous wall. Where the ground levels above Grisedale Tarn the wall ends. From the end of this wall a very thin path traverses around Grisedale Tarn under Seat Sandal to Grisedale Hause. (1 mile)

(Should the gradient of this descent from the metal post be off putting, keep to the main path which descends down to the outflow of Grisedale Tarn. Try keeping to the original zigzags of this path; this not only makes the descent easier but also avoids eroding further one of the most eroded paths in the Lake District. From the outflow of the tarn pick up the old packhorse route to Grisedale Hause. This particular route will add another 200 feet of climbing to the walk, at a point when you will probably be anxious to avoid any climbing whatever - even this slight amount.)

Continued on the next page

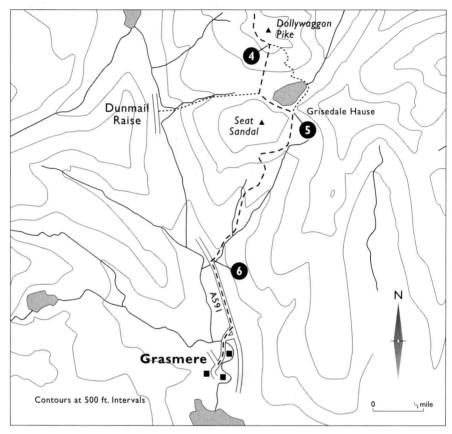

5   From Grisedale Hause follow the old packhorse route southwards. After a quarter of a mile and about three hundred feet of descent carefully note that the original packhorse route veers off to the right from what appears to be the main path, climbing slightly and crossing over a ridge into another valley formed by Little Tongue Gill. This path is much grassier than today's main route and has a better gradient. The path brings you to the main A591, just a few hundred yards from the Traveller's Rest. (1³/₄ miles)

6   Turn left and follow the road to Grasmere. (1 mile)

NB Though this is a very long walk you are not committed to walking the whole length of it as it parallels the 555/6 bus route which runs along the A591, albeit at a somewhat higher level. So if you find yourself running out of time or energy you can always descend westwards to the main road to hail the bus. The two most appropriate paths for an early descent are the paths to Wythburn, descending from the summit of Helvellyn, and to Dunmail Raise, descending from the col between Dollywaggon and Seat Sandal just above Grisedale Tarn. Similarly if you keep to the suggested route you can hail the bus as soon as you reach the A591 near to the Traveller's Rest. This saves twenty minutes walking time back to Grasmere.